Songs for Eurydice

– Stride –

SONGS FOR EURYDICE
First edition 2004
© Keith Jafrate 2004
All rights reserved

ISBN 1 900152 91 6

Cover design by Neil Annat
Cover painting: 'Yoga Fire' [1978] by Alan Davie
Used by kind permission of the artist

Published by
Stride Publications
11 Sylvan Road, Exeter
Devon EX4 6EW
England

www.stridebooks.co.uk
Produced by Bookchase (UK) Limited
L.D.: SE-3714-2004 in Spain
Printed in Spain

Songs for Eurydice

Keith Jafrate

for Ian

best wishes

and many thanks

Keith

Acknowledgements

Parts of this poem were first published in the following magazines, pamphlets and anthologies: *Birdsong* (Spout Publications), *First Draft* (Albert Poets), *Left Curve, Rustic Rub, Scratch, Spout, Tears In The Fence, The Song Of Orpheus* (Slow Dancer Press).

Special thanks to David Caddy, John Harvey and Mark Robinson, three writers who, as editors, have been particularly kind to me over the years.

'Birdsong' and 'At Cerne Abbas' were written as part of a commission from Bedford Readers & Writers Festival, and first performed in Bedford on 24th May 1993 by Robin Hayward (tuba), Paul Hession (drums), Mary Oliver (vocals), Daniel Weaver (cello) and myself on saxophones and vocals.

Lines 1 – 311 of *The Song of Orpheus* were written as part of a commission from Jazz Action in 1994. From these, six *Songs for Eurydice* were derived, and performed at a variety of locations in 1995 by Sang Octet: Robin Hayward (tuba), Paul Hession (drums), Cheryl Martin (vocals), Jakki Perkins (vocals), David Pitt (bass), Simon Pugsley (trombone), Jon Whitfield (drums) and myself on saxophones.

My thanks to all the musicians for their talents and tolerance.

'Body Lyrics' was commissioned by Kunstfabrik, Potsdam, as a daily journal to the public art festival, *Outdoor*, held in Potsdam in the summer of 1996. Parts were then included in the performance *Der Gesang des Stotterers / The Stutterer's Song*, written for and first performed on 31st August 1996 at the *From Orient to Occident Festival* at Cultural Exchange Station Tabor, in the Czech Republic. My thanks to Thomas Kumlehn, with whom I collaborated on both projects. The live recording of *Der Gesang des Stotterers* made in Tabor was released on a CD in 1997 by Edition Instabile Medien.

It is we who built the palaces and cities here in Spain and in America and everywhere. We, the workers, can build cities to take their place. And better ones – we are not in the least afraid of ruins.
– Buenaventura Durruti

In my view, the best works of the contemporary spirit come from the irrational, while what prevails in the world, what dominates and often kills, does so always in the name of Reason. The irrational as a nonbeginning of this project was my starting point.
– Daniel Libeskind

Praise is defiance.
– Margaret Atwood

for Dianne

part 1 *a magical submission*

I blunder towards your kiss like a survivor from a burning house

dusk on the sea
a settling
a loss of footprints
waves paint silver
where light darkens and splits

to walk at the edge of death
to walk on death's tongue
with the thought of your smudged face up close
your shoulders in the half-light
where light is never still
my words resist you
wrestling with gypsy arab butterfly statue

the heart has no space
has the mouth of a whale
sometimes of a shark
can be named and re-named
simpler to say
close my mouth with your mouth
hide my fear with your body

and dream of flame
and dream of flight
where the sea tears open
and I walk open
like a flag to its message
with no one to read me
to myself which signal

do you read me?
the sea collapses like an exhausted sprinter

•

goldwoman
           nefertiti
amber sister
your eyes burnt earth
your eyes
        the exact colour of eyes
remembered on the wings of a butterfly
your laugh hasn't changed
for a thousand years

I go to you
        as to death
meaning
        an assent
a season entered
to keep faith
           with the common flower
call it lipstick
the poppies lipstick the garden

•

your candour lights me
your unbroken face
like a stript branch
like light behind birches
and whatever your mouth is like
grooved like a leaf on your face

where the hearth sits
where law rots
a thousand years and
language inches forward
its source what remains
of a statue
the line of a hip
of a shoulder
their loyalty

so I must sing
as if I read stone
as if I spoke sand
I must sing you back
from the ordinary world

of part of the garden
of the torture of fences
with occasional music
of the paws of the sun
across this writing
with occasional magic
and days of abrasion
of the gifts of water
of the dreams of water
ox-eye daisies
and the gold of your hair
still in the hairbrush

the stones sing me a single note
in the tall flowers accident of bellmetal
faint faint
the sky sings me its envy
of the motions of flesh
the rain is a brush
laid on a cymbal

•

the day smoke-blue
moors drift out of haze
wishing you and *history*
come from the same language
only making stories will unite them

our duty to inhabit all of english
chanteuse of the elder tree
into humid day
the house opens
strong with scents
of paint and timber
and the warm stone
under rain

slow clouds
and a jet's slow scrape
away from here
I try flowers
I try recipes
I try the pinching stones
other traps
that cannot matter
who are friends
marks on my hand
their weight easy
and without hours

I would enter time like a stone
enter stone like a fern

•

the sea is ours
say the gulls
pacing the tide's turn
straitlaced

quick swifts
touch its privacy

the land is smoke
points and piers deep mauve
the seafront poses for a photograph
of Anywhere, Europe

I gather four fragments
of the sea's construction:
stone
      shell
glass
      brick
each drawn into its curved
and moving world
their shapes clarified
by motion to likeness
their colours released
from distraction wholly
different
I give you these metaphors

easy census of similes
of their failure
the language chrome
meaning disease

tonight the wind pours in the trees
opens the wounds of this house
and I study solitude
like a child by a dead bird

I am here
without you
and you so far away
I cannot imagine the furniture

only your face
your fingers
I cannot picture the clothes you wear
there at the border

your nakedness
walks in my dream
out of the distance
like a moment of fear

here in the hard bed
the city a reminder of slammed doors
and voices calling
I enter the water

of sleep
of waiting
my heart falls
my voice stone

•

the dead crowds of the river want to speak to you
the dead crowds of the river batter with lump hammers at the bedroom wall
as you dance on my body
the dead crowds of the river
under dripping blue torches
surround the house with gantries
and watch our love as though it were chess

they touch me with your fingers
they shift you with my hands
the dead crowds of the river
rivet our astonishment to the walls of their dreams
as we gasp and mutter
they carry us like water in their black hands
the hoarse dead of the river drink us
in their racketing eternity
we lie like silence
we build nothing
with careless precision
we embrace and sleep

(rage in the cavern under striplights
to vomit whole icecubes and wooden bricks and husbands
and every scrap of every accoutrement broken by all of us
revenge sex and the shouting foreplay
how we are trapped and must fuck among concrete
door not to be freed
vault not to be battered with anything containing bone
each heart and soul I vomit and my fear
of the future's cold confinement)

all words fall
into each other flunk-daft
little in carpet dust
he-and-squeaking picture of myself
on the back of your corpse

over the fading picture of your face
my want of what has vanished
into cold streets like a siren
now it is silent
to insert our gentleness into eternity
a match-flame after the sun has died

•

should I resist these lines
dragged from me at midnight
by a nothingness?

I tested my prayer at many altars
only you answer
I swam beyond the wall of our bodies
and back to my dream of you
should I resist these lines?
should I turn to sleep
as to a housewife?
should I lick the blood of verbs
as it pours from my hand
my hand which has held you
which writes these lines?

the sea falls white
on the black shore

tonight your image
possesses me like rage
should I resist these lines
dragged from me at midnight?

•

I have read my own story
you are the victim of its joy

in it my heart builds
a temperate house

a place in myself
outside the weather

between murder and desire
no house

no border
I twist

the kaleidoscope
to show you

the man who obeys each clerk
and beats his wife

where the damned must spend eternity talking
and every word they say

must be a lie
where the clock is handcuffed

where torture is to look
at beauty

I have been writing this poem for a thousand years
from an idea a thousand years forming

now I open it like a broken factory
to fireweed

song step into the flame of her hair
song
take the swarm of my wounds to honey her
dance for the map of scars
humming-bird song
arrive from the blur of your heart's disintegration
instantly to glitter in a pelt of lakes
make her laugh as if death had forgiven us
bring leaves bring salt
show her the forest of the city
show her the slow flight of stones
show her all that is impossible
imagined in your singing

song
magical submission
hunt in her the gift of change
do not be finished
do not be finished
begin song
begin your journey in my voice
begin your perfect forgetfulness
let her catch in you the lie of music
let her see time

part 2 *the descent beckons*

I renounce my cruelties
I renounce the cage of my cruelties
I renounce the need to return
I renounce the need to promise

I renounce the virus of images
the crowd in my dreams I relinquish
I relinquish the excuse of hate
the justification by anger
I renounce the hollowness of anger

I renounce the grief of toil
I renounce the friendship of uncertainty
I renounce the fear of conviction
I am convicted
I have paid
it is over
I renounce my cruelties

I am clean for the journey
on a day of rain
a long-legged fly
trembling at my window

the house ticks and whispers
riding a calm

all is new
this pain is new

love was an integument of gongs
a dream we fought to wake from

what have I murdered
remembering?

dull fist
ants crawl on my secrets

daisy petals
and how the wind decides

no favours
here is the door

take my hand
where love is love's torture

the first room:
nude mannequins
ghosts with bandaged hands
holding photos of lovers
the walls all doorways
dead joyriders lugging rusty bazookas
hordes who died in lycra
compelled to shriek with laughter
only their eyes left to their own control
speak in that language which longs to speak
or dream
watching the jerk of themselves in others

they do not know you're there
her voice wakes me
this prepares them

for the honeycomb of babies
each with a tie-clip microphone
on the pinched skin of their chests
the walls black with loudspeakers
speakers everywhere on black plinths
the scream is an arriving missile
I feel the pipes inside me move and cringe
brakes of a million rusting engines
it is impossible to run here
these are not dead
thin high-pipe flute voice
passes beside me

how these are imaginings
thoughts of the new
they wait without digestion
they are always hungry
always alive
you are not enough to feed them

and then the hangar of faulty striplights
no rhythm to the flicker
fathers and mothers yellow-grey
on bare concrete
everywhere the figures in lab coats
hold out meters to measure the moaning
they stoop in polite attention
none may shout here none
may speak the language of their neighbour
they whisper as we pass
bee-drone of anguish
side-mouthed repetitions
where are our daughters?
none may sleep here
only exchange photographs
they raise dog-eared visas
ripped passports as we pass
they believe in elsewhere she murmurs

then the endless exhibition of sitting rooms
men masturbate
holding tiny photographs

some with tiny televisions
their pricks impetigo red
hands slowing
down speeding-up
wordless questioning noises
and some openly weeping
like absurd machines
they will never come is all she tells me
so many rooms
enough for two mirrors
turned to face each other
none are cursed here
they have only lived

and then darkness
a bridge on a dirt road
we walk into cold
lit mist tang
of metal shriek
of bloated jets above
that fall to a white blaze in the distance
the mist fills me
I am blind with its colours
dragged hanging onto her coat
over the river
white light through chainlink
silhouettes of claw and man-high wheels
scarred ice black in cut mud
we enter a field full of silver

shivering
the sound of shivering
pillars of glass and among them women
men gagged their hands
chained to their ankles
stare through blue glass at each other
and shuffling the pallid avenues
woodlice big as dogs
investigate these lovers who cannot move
one rears against me
its stomach a loom of clicking tendons
its jaws clacking like woodblocks
harmless she whispers
smooth and hesitant
the lice move on their rails
twitching over backs and thighs
and everywhere the shivering
the shivering
eye locked to eye they endure
these are lives the plague has entered
my senses blacken
and block with refusal
jamming these image with fire
the touch of your breast on my arm in darkness
with the heat of your eyes
I pray for the breathing of cattle
for colour
as my hands flatten the front of my eyes I see them
you must consent

it wasn't me
IT WASN'T ME
and if it was?

image of you
naked in peat
your skin streaked with dirt
long grasses sodden flat
follow your curves
as if you were their motion
or you the earth's gesture
your hair slick with mud
on your right side eyes shut
still under the rain
that patterns your body
hands in your lap
the sole of one foot turned back
to face us

your lips
mauve
are your lips
your fingers
thin and feathered against mud
like an unearthed carving
are your fingers
your hair pulled back
shows your slender neck
your slender neck in the wet ditch

yet you read this
as I stare down at you
floating under the page
night or day
you read this

no trees in the hedgerows
cold land shining under moonlight
ache of stars

bring a small light
as of a torch through fingers

bloodlight
to warm the image I found
in the earth of my own mind

in the bones of my poem
I sing to wake Eurydice
who was dead to me

how was she killed how often was she killed?
by the cold
by language

I must drift to the mouth of language
with your picture burning

I must not look back
till we are home

your face
your shoulders
beginning

part 3 *a little song of rain*

all the songs fall past your face
all the silences of all earth's tongues
fall from the years into this stillness

loose like a forest
like a forest where graves hide
(should I read or dance?)
like a forest where tiny blue flowers
entrap the general
listen
rain whispers through its muffled timbales
with all the rhythms of the earth:

the dead are gone
Antonio is gone
Margaret is gone
we know only their fear
we meet them in the living

Anna has gone
Asa has gone
as you walk through fern towards me
the wood around us waiting
in the distance a handsaw like the panting of a dog

part four: *bird song*

hunting the smoke of you
your skill as a ghost
in the funhouse of the past

all those lies that run below language
I must tell them out loud
I must shatter them like dolls

we who were once priests
now play for butchers
bow to the heart's dwarves

your verse broken to build slogans
so many days since this song touched you
I must practise as if without hands

beyond the luscious secrecy of trees
we who were once priests
climb to the stunt window

turn dream to hammers
blow the raw sea into flowers
esperanto of sirens

the search abolishes itself
the hunt for love
the marvellous digressions of cloud

the imagined space called *heart*
like the past imagined
made of junk and wishes

heat comes into the leaves
their last choler

you'll arrive
nothing can stop it
out of the earth's mouth

addicted to sleep
the earth rolls into fire

the wine talks to itself on the sideboard
of berries and frost

the echo of loss
the form of all loss
seconds waste away like ice on fast water

with a corpse to exchange for your belief
that cannot sing
or dream or fail or speak

    black
    bird

    yellow
    beak

    green
    leaf

    red
    berry

the sparrow is beside us
flying through fences
through sour violence of nightfall
by the shattering of concrete
the sparrow never thinks for us
twitching a moment at the gutter and gone
and beside us
the sparrow is beside us empty
calling through luggage
to the skin that covers us
forgetful and ravenous
on the cold rail
on the metal road
rain makes tiny necklaces
on the window
land of ochre and verdigris
trees soaking into grey sky

and the sparrow flying
like a leaf in the wind
leafage of monuments and runways
her skin all leaves
beside us

the skulls of cars
our appetite for mud
a mattress assassinated by a blank embankment
red ink of cartons washed to tan
by smog-wash and oil and our faith in acid
beside the rot of crust and wrapper
rich pickings on the vomit trail
whatever the daylight
whatever morality has failed

beside us
the sparrow is empty
her ricochet empty
of your mouth's soft method

where the beads and pearls
and droplets run together
on this glass
a silver net over daylight
made of our breathing
as the circle closes
you clear a circle on the window
to look at morning

    black bird
    yellow beak

    green leaf
    red berry

to bless this extremity
that can see no use for itself but torment
stoned on the thirteenth floor
obsessed with defending obsession
the river at night an absence under the window
a ravine of darkness in the christmas city
shall we declare war on one-another
and prepare for the end of the world?
I was invented by a fatal disease
trees observe me
small birds come
small songs and snatches
at the fresh fruit museum
where the damned buy poison
each leaf carefully poisoned
to suppress the madness of sanity
where pain is consumption
at the racks you protect me
by the chilled dreams
where clerks whisper
each song a bird baffled
a gull flung above the river
where traffic interrupts

in day-bile and night's weight
meat onto flowers
the name full of pins like a toy mouse
that was dead and lost its name
blood lost its name to ink
on the high bridge
where the wind has broken its last restraint
and pours through the heart a dead river
a blade of dead water hammered out upstream
from ghost-fires
and the squirt of every necessary process
that maintains this blindness

to lay down our speeches in a sloping garden
to dig and cut till the world ends
sharing games and refusals
to be the treasurers of blue
to be the stone that will never read itself
to be the builders
to be the last

to lay down my speeches
in the summer of your body
to turn from the world
and see how at your eyes
the sun has made a valve of floating mothwing
bronze underwater armour
a bark of light

        black bird
        yellow beak

        green leaf
        red berry

only wasted shapes
irrecoverable gee-gaws
how they've set wheels to the trap
and air clatters
harder and harder to believe

> *from the end of the world*
> *greetings*
> *greetings to the infinity of displacements*
> *greetings to the packed silence of time*
> *to dust and ice*
> *greetings to fire*
> *and the lightless immensities that soak fire up*
> *greetings to the inexhaustible web of starlight*
> *to acid and shooting star*
> *to darkness*
> *to the massive slow falling from nothing to nothing*
> *greetings*
> *from the first discoverers of blood*
> *this song and its mathematics*
> *this witness*

let the kitchen travel through immensity
its light shining out
its exit towards silver
the grass burnt black in circles
at the lip of the city
five magpies walk in contemplation

of how not to serve
how best to work

how truth is a worm
nothing like this song

how time shines in you like dancing
how we search for music

madness of numbers
madness of tongues
un stylo the children whisper
m'sieur un stylo
give me a pen
to unlock the stone
the builder imprisoned by percentages
the house on a wave's hill
your face its lamp

in this poison land
on a humpback bridge
alone with the cooling towers

sieved acres
coffee-dark and black
gulls and bulldozers
chunks of water left in pits

the victims of double-glazing
their decaying towns
surrounded by poison

a tip of shattered concrete
on the wire
rags of polythene show the wind's temper

part 5 *at Cerne Abbas*

soft motioning space bigger than a dream of ocean
dark inside darkness
that has consumed all forests
infinity of wheels in collapsing green
honeycomb inside honeycomb inside honeycomb
sleep flight into surf
containing every change contained by change

>   to see the different heights of death that grow with you:
>   the sea where you drown
>   and the wise bastard with the poisonous watches

>   it's lonely and there's no scenery

cathedral of shadows
where the birds can't be frightened
ageless orchard of the dreaming present
where every sound comes filtered through water

>   it's lonely and there's a man talking
>   he knows your trap and describes it

dark valley gold meadows
the eye tilts falling over burnt sierra
this landscape of fur for your body
that curls sleeping like a river

your toes reach the ocean
a mountain your pillow
feathered with forest
these memories from another place
this sound a single clear horn

    small as an eardrum
    shuttling big as a turbine
    pressing his verbs on the tearducts
    kitchen knife he says and *kickin*
    and *wooncha wanna killim?* he says

    how the moon is a face and the fist is a world
    how the blade is a world and the world is lead
    how the world is glass and the eye is a globe
    how the globe is a heel and the mouth is a world
    how the seed is a world and the world a needle
    how the world is a pain and the pain a planet
    stuck in the gullet the world is a bone
    is a bone smoothed down and carved for a blade
    how death is a world and the world is dead
    lying down in the nerves that make each fist
    how the world is a door and the cage is a world
    how the voice is a cage and the cage a story
    how the whisper kills and the word is dead
    how death is a house and the furniture death
    how the house is a jail and the jail a fire
    burning the tenderness out of a man
    how a man is a world and the world is lost
    turning and turning and turning and turning

        it's lonely
        he says *I wanna stabber 'nfuck the-ole*

        and I say it
        in the hot dark

falling towards darkness
searching years into darkness
sifting and turning
how dust turns and clay at the rivermouth
like high grey feathers of cloud
flower of starlings on the faded city
falling in an element that blends all elements
fire burning through water
air torn by a thousand bells
passing through earth through fire passing
again and over again through darkness
where nothing touches
where light touching a fragment makes distance visible
where everything is distant falling
falling

I have wanted to thaw this pain
pierce the hillside with my eyes
meet my opponent with a weapon of grass
to be the song within riot
to be here
I have wanted to be here
within the siren

within electricity
within the earth
the earth within

earth is my prison
time is my prison
the hill my window
I see through stone
from the time of villages
I pursue this future
running against you
I must break the silence
trapped in your noise
make music of the motion of water
the broken voice of dirty rivers
how we fill each other's eyes like clouds on water
my song must break this drifting
to say your single fingernail supports all history
here in the scar on your elbow every journey
I will never be new
only perhaps my singing will make you remember
I must stamp on silence in the roar of grass
how the wind hisses there like hot metal
dipped into rusty water
which is my song
within the hot nerves of numbers
my rusty voice lies unrecorded
a figment lost in monoxide

I do not know what the world is
to be driven naked from the hills
my symbols useless and laughable

words kill me
names I can't keep
fenced in or out

I do not come with murder
I do not come with the magic of law
that tells you where you stand

you cannot stand
that you stand nowhere
without torment

I do not come with words closed into houses
into books and envelopes and cables
I come to stand here forever

by the quivering flowers
by the supple water
where words start

I come from the beginning of colours
from the door you think is sealed
from everywhere

I see through stone
I see through time
I come to enter you

see with your eyes
have you forgotten
we are sons and daughters

we came from desire
our time is desire

part 6 *ghost tribunal*

have you walked in the world without fear?
I have sat in the café by the water
beside its narrow window
to watch the water crease like beaten metal
where the light burns out all shape
burning white and blue and gold
and showing again the grey water
where waves tick past the window
and light leaks from their crests
into burning flat whiteness
that blinds the window
replacing its perspective
with a wall of white and gold
quivering and merging
quivering and moving apart
where the small waves nod and march
I have left my eyes open
where light burns a doorway
out of the water
a shape without depth
with the water beyond it
so the room is a sound
coming out of the light
where I see only light
in the flaming window
where I sit by the window

eyes wide open
perfectly open

traffic comes to the light and waits
and passes on
the halted drivers facing forward
distracted by the placing of a frame
around dusk
do not look aside
we do not look at them too long
the passenger on buses also
do not look aside
until each bus moves off
for this is fear
and sometimes a man his one arm
slack outside the car will stare
as a fed cat will stare
and then more rare than this
the face we cannot name

you
the audience
grow impatient

hush and drone of motors
teenagers passing on foot to the hot town
stare at us from their limited wisdom
through the window
in our tableau of interruption

with the cut of brakes
background of haste and interference
this is the place where you hear me
there is no other
do not listen past this place for that pure space
where the poem is beaten clear
where the poem endures without ghosts
where that longed-for face has come and been catalogued
flower
fearless entanglement
like the eye of no other animal
neither dream nor myth
I danced by the jaws of fear like a child
and the fear relented and grew blind
I sang before the kings of pain

(on the bus the breadwinners
and their children
are slack and slightly important
a man with a large round head
adjusts the collar
of his velour shirt
in the dark glass behind the driver
a woman watching him
as if he were a dog
in clothes is still
as the bus swaggers off uphill)

words like bees
like children from a broken school
dive into the world like birds
like blossom sliding on the wind's shoulder
our narrative digresses
but does not escape
where the story is fear
its need to be told to be finished
its need of motion
its way of arranging objects
the veins on a leaf or a fly's wing
that endanger its sanity
unless given purpose
the veins of a tree in December
the veins of its reflection
unless set in motion
the story is the need of stories
which has become our enemy
the flower which has become our enemy
like the skin of a face
like the powdered skin of my mother's face
like the skin of a baby's face
which is neither skin nor face
but white of daisies
and certain kinds
of silk

which has become our enemy
its sabotage imagined where language
like a broken jetplane
smashes into pollen and scatters
leaving troops to collect the wreckage
to reassemble the sentence
imagine its last moments
of sense
before the flower bent over Manhattan
before the flower yawned on Hong Kong
panic in the streets of Mexico City
where the flowers nod like stoned dancers
and cannot march
the narrative needs motion
the system needs motion

on the pale grey of the platform
snails are sailing

past clipped fields under cooling towers
their vast exhalations unfolding together
above the black block
black barrows of coal
sky comes low to graze the towers
skim the steam into its sliding
a small train practises rhythms
moderato past the poisoned cows
where we two walk downhill
out of the story

to sip from the rip-saw grass
with safe tongues
where the painting pours its bottle-green grass
into our mouths
and the painter paints gills on our necks
wings on our backs

•

but in the ghost land no one farms
false hills slip under sharp grass
ditches run black and orange
at the edge of water and suburbs
past abandoned gardens
of the new estates
dusk and the land vanishes
into underwater silt of mist

no one comes from the city
to this city without walls
no one rambles past the tanned palisades
only the train removes us
past a scorched earth cold as death
each turf without pressure
of centipede or worm inside it
each field pestless and slack
its birth a commodity of green levers
in this theory of weather
midwinter icemare without so much as a greenfly
no brilliance in the leaves of new wheat
abandoned here like strangers
to shiver outside spring's oven

or silence would fall with the snow
but for a thousand trapped engines
that rage where the lilac
stick its hip through a white tunic
the plough scrapes downhill out of blindness

53

silence would make itself visible in mittens
of snow on each fold of the cypresses

iron beats in the world, behind snow that brings its gloved performers in a panto about
objects, the biscuit world arriving gently like reality falling asleep, gently sleep swells
the litter of timber, affecting what was thrown to be burnt with a decisiveness, some
latent design only the painter could see before this snow arrived, painters walk up the
hill carrying shiny white bags, the bus ferries them past composing

dusk falls
like a roomful of moths

no pictures of torment will satisfy these shades
their punctuation
its steady
unsyncopated march
on ghost land
marked like a treasure map
with mutineers
a captain of good
country stock:
we must rebel to exist
to count in the story
its foregone conclusion

to enter the collective of language
where no extreme will measure us
a bombed abattoir full of snow
ten billion assassins

will not measure us
defeated by clerks
their phrases like stones
used to press words from human toys
like a doll with its own tiny doll
nothing mothered or loyal

Thank you for your letter of July 14th, the implications of which I am rather concerned by. You appear to be objecting to the stipulation on behalf of the funding organisations that a monthly report should be made by the co-ordinator to them as funders, an objection which I find strange to say the least. All clients of local authorities and arts boards are accountable to their funders. This is all the more so with a development agency which (in terms of management if not in terms of employment law or conditions) is more analogous to an employee than a client. Quite apart from this it is the feeling of both the local authority and myself that we have had difficulty in the past because of a lack of a single contact within the area. This is partly for the benefit of the constituency but also as a figure answerable to the funders for projects undertaken. We did try to express this at the meeting you refer to. I have to be clear now that our continued funding is absolutely contingent on the co-ordinator role being filled in a satisfactory manner, and part of this post would be to make a monthly report to the funders.

the mad are sincere
saving us from innocence

to be beaten over and over
in imagination's anger

unless we make art
soft war like snow over junkyards

and the rain that unpicks stone
who were beaten by language

unless we make stories
how flame crashed from our wishes

flying to sense like music
without law or permission

to be fucked over and over
in m'lady's chamber

unless we make anger
from the scraps of memoranda

unchain ourselves from brevity
and curse

and here? well, it's a weird world. john from the corner theatre asked me if i wanted to perform on their stage in a city-sponsored outdoor rock and arts festival. i said, sure. then he calls up to try to talk me out of it, saying i won't get paid. i go, that's okay. then he says, you can't use profanity, because it's a family-oriented festival. i go, no problem, never curse anyway. then he says, no one will understand you; you'll go over their heads. i go, i don't care, i do it for me. then he says, you'll be too political, you'll be uncomfortable. i listen to him, and i think, isn't it amazing when the cultural underground internalizes mainstream conservatism, and then tries to marginalize its own people. i thought that was the job of the police, in a manner of speaking. i say to him, no problem, i've been silenced enough, i'll perform. forward to the barricades!

to let my hands remember
holding timber
certain scars you can't abolish
and dreams that return over and over
holding a shovel

a thousand years to make water free
a thousand years at the kerbside
in half-naked gangs
to remember wheatfields
orchards passed in a crew-bus
to remember how they work
as if in a daydream to straighten
and realise in the ditch
this road leads nowhere
while across the fence
beyond the wall
she beckons like a sea
like the running of a sea

      the lion grass
running to gold
      giant mane
of earth's shaking
      head-dress dance
beyond notation
      running lost
improvisation of this wind

        beyond sense
slow hiss of infinite cymbals
        beyond sense
decisions of air decisions of water
        beyond sense and substance
into words
        the fear comes
like a sound half-heard
        the stone of fear falls
like a hammering behind walls
or soft as smoke
but clear as the faint collision
of a key in its lock
the fear runs into me
like wind in a limp shirt
image of pleading handless cuffs
in the sunny garden
the stone of fear stares
spits
and talks again by the jacked-up car
as if time were a weight
hung over my body

to fill with a boy's sorrow
playing the-man-with-the-gun
shooting himself as a child
his brothers and teachers by the mainline
cutting down old birches
their heart-wood like pale butter
where the may flowers

in the daylight comes to me this flashback
let the words join how they will
this descent to the cold among children
  let the words join
without images of pain
so that pain is forced into hips and knees
it pours into matter
  denied voice
the pain returns as worn bone
to make age an image of pain
and language simplifies again to hunger
and revulsion
  desire
and rejection
  hunger
and decay
as childhood decays into language
words extend to shadow blankness
in the daylight comes to me this winter
in the morning this darkness
this blazing conception of chaos
which is the boy alight inside me
who saw without defence of habit
and returns to be born

•

in the sun the shadow
of a bus passing

dusk after light
dusk after light

a spider struggles on the speckled lino
dragging two broken legs

the sound of the broken spider imagined
as wholeness
        not imperfection
or nostalgia for silk
the word of the broken weaver
thundering without term or deadline
forever in this poem
        to sing it
to suffer its terror and fact
to grip its torment like a song
claw of jets on the sky's wall
drag of rust under each ton
that each step has become
each metal mouth of the fact
of death's snapshot
        sing it

I am broken motion towards infinite falling
my little body through fabric of images
where we imagine limits through privacy
of species or universe I am broken motion
to that space which has ceased to be space
and anywhere I sing little fearless hymns
to touch the dust of everyone again
as I have from such a dream curved out
and back imagined motion while nowhere
everywhere I part and cover all that differs
and returns to energy its loan its print
its song of me in the memory of is

the moment of leaving
always confused with loss
the trains leave without fuss
sound of knife-grinders
going about their business

Something has changed, fundamentally. This is evident. What is it? Before, they all wanted to be the ploughmen of history, to play the active parts, each one of them to play an active part. Nobody wished to be the manure of history. But is it possible to plough without first manuring the land? So ploughmen and manure are both necessary. In the abstract, they all admitted it. But in practice? Now something has changed, since there are those who adapt themselves philosophically to being manure, who know this is what they must be and adapt themselves. You only live once, as the saying goes; your own personality is irreplaceable. You are not faced abruptly with an instant's choice on which to gamble, a choice in which you have to evaluate the alternatives in a flash and cannot postpone your decision. Here postponement is continual, and your decision has continually to be renewed. This is why you can say that something has changed. There is not even the choice between living for a day as a lion, or a hundred years as a sheep. You don't live as a lion even for a minute, far from it: you live like something far lower than a sheep for years and years and know that you have to live like that.

swallows silent as their own shadows
weave over the weaving river
plough a dust of mosquitoes

five ducks work against the current in a line

to enter the world as a witness
not as the world itself
a mistake
eating trout with almonds
or this wine
in a place named in the world
in a room with a named use
where names turn
like frightened fish and won't be still
and cannot join
names and the shadows of names
entering the world unfinished
and without the power to complete themselves
torn away from the fire of the world

becoming our names
begun beyond memory of naming
in the imagination of beginnings

while rain names the night
strong with scent of stone

and in the clattering morning
the languages flash like wagtails
with their dipping flight
around the tables
words essay their identities
flicker above memory like flies
above the fast river
where trout rise to take them

but not to have looked at you enough
not to have been entered
by landscape's shadows at evening
on the cinnamon earth between vines
their green braids ranged on its shoulders
to have spent life passing
in the stillness of dawn
when the bird's purity has no hindrance
in a lane under trees
where the tarmac dies away
to run out of road
and the desire for motion
and the desire for language

so I must sing
where the trees step into morning
I must sing with their rhythm
as a witness to the end of measure
where the trees dance as if waking
I have come to your face
your body that listens
that returns from language
neither true nor broken
to enter the song like a secret
an air in the leaves that leaves describe

I (Orfeo)
to be leaf
sing
cascade of wounds in flicker passing
under my tongue
I (Orfeo)
arrive at your body
your face turned aside
your lips are moving
no words there

part 7 *the song of orpheus*

when flowering things
when flowering
things flowering things when

when flowering
things when flowering
when things flowering
flowering flowering
when things
when things flowering when
flowering

flowering things things flowering when
flowering when flowering things
things when flowering
when things flowering

rain
making
in the chestnut
clouds
in the silt river skin
into flowering
watermarks
and the strong wind-
stream through canes

in September
when fall flowering
flowering things
when flowering things fall
what will you do?

the slow waves of trees shift
leaves push gold into the light
light flowering fall to gold
to gold waves shift and push when
fall flowering waves of light shift
into light push into waves' shift fall
flowering gold when waves fall
into shift in fall light
waves gold and flowering
when flowering flowering things
in waves fall flowering

where I was cold was
death no enemy death
no enemy enemy death
no I was cold where
enemy I was no enemy
to death where cold was no enemy was
where I was enemy to death death
spoke no cold was where I enemy
to enemy was cold to death death
spoke cold enemy to cold where I
was death no was I enemy I

spoke to death death spoke flowering
September was my return
my no where light waves

into waves into cold
light waves where
gold death leaves push
waves into flowering where death
shifts into water
marks the edge of possible
light things flowering things
fall flowering after rain
remember

remember
in the mountain in the leaf
in the valley in the leaf
careful terracing where no fields match
like a hand in the mountain remember

leaves like shavings of white
yellow light discarded wardance
armour stained
glass birdbreast leaves
the tree remembers
flowering to lose these windows
lit by dream of flowering release
to fall from pain's place
peach yellow dream away

from where the tine enters
spine needle pining into dream
of flowering flowering how
like a harmless claw fall
flowering all pain's images
to dream remembering what
is and hidden gold hand
into the mountain's leaf of
river terracing in waves fall
possible slow possible things
flowering remember pain spoke clear
to push death where the tine
spine needle fear-like-
nothing grows no-possible-
flowering flowering things
discarded where the chair
is pain wall pain is
window floor is pain where
pain wins fear like
spine needle tine to
door in pain pain flowering
flowering rain in the mountain
remember in pain flowering
the valley flowering in
pain in flowering fall flowering
things things birdbreast lightdance flowering

where the souls scream for life
where the souls from cages
of labour scream for life
where the souls in their cage of years
years scream for life more life
where the souls scream for
freedom freedom where the souls
like conscious birds scream life
for life where the souls scream
in their cage of betrayal scream
freedom freedom where things
scream flowering flowering souls
scream for life where the souls
in their wreckage of blood burn scream
scream to be free more life
to scream flowering fall freedom
freedom to life where the souls
scream in light to love light to
love flowering in scream to be
free where freedom where the souls
dream of life in pain's chair
waves of pain where the screams
for life in waves fall flowering
flowering not to be me
no longer be me but free
but free from cages cages flowering
in cages where the souls
long not to be to be
freedom freedom

under flower cage mountain
where time follows time like leaves like
birdbreast tree-feather time
where time like time like
flowering like time where the chair
is time wall time is
window floor is time where rain
makes the roofs white
where the blackbird's warning echoes

where the sun
slides down itself
out of clouds like dust

where the clouds point west
torn by the wind
into trails and ribbons

where hate falls like snow
where hate lies like snow
where hate like snow falls
hate like snow falls
no matter what eyes what ears
where hate hears like snow
all possible possible flowering
falls all snow remember
water and the wind-
stream through canes
like snow flowering

of snow remember all falls
like hate no matter
what eyes what hears all
possible possible lightdance
snow remember where
snow hate lies or memory of snow
is hate and future
hate falls hate lies hate
lies snow all memory
of snow like lies lies
snow lies like hate all
falls like matter eyes all
falls flowering hears snow
like snow or memory of snow
or possible snow hate
where hate lies like snow

where the soil hates
where the flower hates
pain where hate looks at the flower
at the picture hate breathes hate
calls in the room
in the room like a mask
locked on the world
hate like a mask
locked on the world the voice
locked on the world
and dreamless dreamless accurate

when flowering
things fall flowering snow
to unmake facts and likenesses
when snow falls flowering
to cover the litter of days with silence
flowers of silence
making names and the love of names
making the names of love
and love's likenesses
snow falls
flowering to be
love's emblem
lightdance birdbreast flowering
where the chair is love
wall love is window floor is love where
snow like love falls flowering
difference like snow leaves
time in flowering
to fall love rain makes
things fall snow of leaves of snow
and the trees like ink
rest on the distance

like fins of the flying world like
hands sifting rain from rain from
jewellery of rain and bud
swell fingers undersea sifting
sun from rain like
giant hands to

skein the light in wings
of rain and powder sun
of giant hands that pouring light
let colour stand like trees
of ribbon stained
glass skeins of feather light
light sifting veins to fall
like undersea silk blood fin fall
flowering flowering

music where the bees pass
under wet sheets on a line
how the world is crammed
with clear threads of music
music in that place where water
can't see itself beside the railway
talking and the birds
those orators
who solve things by music
and the rain
by music adds its useless useless music
to the earth

I am by the window
there is a colour of music falling
like the stones have blushed
and the road
chuckles with waves
of waves of music

talking and the birds
birds those
clear threads
flash their silks

idle percussion of white

a man in a yellow waterproof
head back laughing
with crooked teeth
by a hole in the road
snow snow
like blazing wings of light
comes and goes
and the sun remains
music of intentionless yellows

pianissimo music
of clouds of rain rain
descending the ladder of rooftiles turning
wheels of rainsilver music
of abacus rain adding drop by drop to the slope of cables

music of voices
chasing each other like waves
behind waves where trees
find light through each other
flower of voices out of air
guiding air like flowers

to die in the sun our own deaths
where the treetops shine like new cane
silence of everything happening
the purr of worlds in our ears

to die in the sun in our own lives
where dreams pester the shore
to die at the edge of ourselves
like a hand into cobweb
where massive tiny spiders
swing over cities of primrose

music of everything becoming everything
a story told to the dying
so that dying is a chosen dream
a flight over woodland

over moorland over stone
over the surf
rising like bread against this island
into the dark

to feel earth bulge
out into the dark
fibres of light
the sky tender as a black cat

where words fall finally
into gold in turquoise and the dark
blue-black flowering out of light

where the dead lie beyond blindness
heavy and weightless
who live only through dreaming
into flight
soft
harmless stars
where sleep flowers
to dream and make names
to dream and heal stones
to dream a thousand seasons
where the trees like ink
rest on the water
what will you do?
sing the leaves like slow
doors closing over death
dandelion clocks like dusk moons

this only
wall of hands
will do

the only fight is
silent and unfamous
flame but only
what must mean
leaves mean leaves or water
over and over water
over and over
I future you with leaves

or water being leaves a dance
from everywhere to reach
each fingertip of all and touch me
my time

back to earth
how words say it
yellow
impregnable
petals
in the tortured
worker

nothing
only water
calling out of mind
like speech

who did not choose
choosing
who did not know
learning
and all the gardens part of it

a dream that moves
among blow-torch flowers
dream and pain
at the dream's surface
like water stung by flies

a dream inside its mountain
wreckage under dark
water corpse portrait
change escaping
burned flowers nude in the jailhouse
sing like red dresses
in the archive of duckingstools
by the tools of ash
through the gems of pain
the cat licks between paving stones
rubs his head on tufts of dry grass
where each sense is a door
locked and the dream
in cages flowering like elder
flowers between bars
and in the windows of ruins
where the codes war like ants
the stones replaced with pavings
harder than stone

the may flowers melt away
into the leaves like dew
where we have forgotten each other
fighting to remain
where hands have sifted the earth to death
where hands have pressed the earth flat
fearful voices murmuring escape

I have lived in the cage of voices and grown deaf
now all voices are the same to me

a fly lands on the word *hands*

in the rooms of death
in the rooms of glass
to enter light within light
of day after day behind day
tender remembering of light
enters room after room
of speech of messages
echoing wealth of speech
against speech
to find your death within death
like a speech lost in all words spoken
since words were spoken:

a crow and its shadow on the hot roof
falling silent as light

trees rise behind the house
blue shadows breaking green

the tall grass stampedes suddenly
and comes to rest

wide-eyed mouths
flowers shake themselves to pieces

the day will end
but day will not
and beyond day unmoving time
and beyond time the crow at the gutter
blinks like a toy and turns its head

part 8 *by the fire*

all the wars were lost
as it was their nature to be

and now my voice is old
unique among insects

all time has improvised
in the wings of a greenfly

and thought made of wings
detaches from action

I talked
but the blackbird sang

his audience gardens
hidden places

foxes moved into the suburbs
and my life passed

imagining the parliament of flies
which met everywhere

all ways and outside
making fires at night

in a wood in parkland
our picture a small lit space

in a huge lit space
by the modesty of trees

to invent mountains
by measuring ourselves

but how will the dreamers eat?
they will eat like dreamers and thieves

like flies on flowers
praise them

who forget towards death
changing nothing

outside language
outside the firelight

of cities
where time has torn free

from its picture
the wood flies from the park

with every nightfall
outside the light

to make light
and dream ourselves

before this
before always

before the moment of division
we fail to imagine

crude questions:
how will the greenfly choose?

like a greenfly
the loveliest

forget their colours
in the search for space

outside space
where the leaf forms outside change

finite itself as the fountain of leaves
which is tree

its end a seed
a darkness of memory

a concept scarred
that must form again

like a hand in the womb
until nothing

which is all we dream
and was

in the war of language against us
a pattern of loss

an image of reason
in absence

the turquoise wing
clarifying as the fly crawls

in the dark arch under cedars
on long grass

flame green
by a fire at night

the fly travels
into darkness upwards

like a part of dust
its rise and decision

voices make
by the fire

fire gathers
like a tribe

to fight things without fire
levelling

flowering
levelling

bodies fall by the fire's petals
without knowing the fire

we lost one-another
in a darkness of choices

beyond the fire's darkness
in mauve avenues

all the slaveries of light
burning

fire like a door
opens into time

where we lie in the cool grass
asleep in a trap of light

in a trap of light
the moon stares

mesmerised by the city
our hands made

and lost to the hypnotist
capital

in whose wood we make room
with the wrong light

falling on leaves and falling back
like silent water

pouring from the fire
like a white cat caged with a live dove

our senses shrank
to the fire's food

its delicacy stolen
from the flood of numbers

nine or ten
subtract themselves

a cell of astrophiles
but who remembers?

those who look at time
through this time's amber

like a charm worn
in hope of good weather

its truth
a flickering

flower in the dark
whose circle we make

encircled
our food baked in the embers

a small flame
dumb in us

lost like a coin
in a hoard of light

in a hoard of light
hiding from light

in the glittering thrown clutter
of roofs and spaces

in the dust of wheel-ruts and the flattened
cans and shoes and rags of corners

in the necessity for language
where language falls like litter

in the rush and thud below accents
in smoke

the colours given water
in the water of a million windows

in the glass canal
in the mauve towers

in the blue trees
in endlessness

I recognise my city
in the public dreaming of strangers

in the parks at noon
I recognise my city

running from the wood
by landfill where the world is crushed

together elements
smashed and pieces

slung in a bowl of earth
I recognise its silence

crushed and gutted rust
and sawn-mouth waste

of petro-chemical eternities
of coffee grounds and white

scum of reject lubricant
on yard after yard of blue

polythene off-cut stuffed
under crust and solvent

clay on rags and green
oil red water sticklebacks

flicking the red shallows over
paths across gravel

into sand and the gobs
of a dredger supping bedframes

out of silver beer-foam lock pools
by the town of drums

sweet peardrop scent
acids wash into mud

cake caterpillar track petrified
sleeper chewed bridge

by the stuck saplings
by the tin hot sweatshops

blackstone no-garden terraces
under floodlight

torture sleepless trunk roads
from one dead burg to another

in the white night murder
where appetite is blind

eats cunt mince death fun
in the white light anything

club tooth bone
head against head in the white

light over windscreens over
and over

over and finished
and walking alive in my city

I saw all our lives held over
elements crushed without fable

nymphs and shepherds armed to the teeth
with envy

its addiction donated
in return for time

wasted at the frontline
between air and petal

where all autopsies
and shattered

lists of names
reverse the tide

of thought itself
to fire's unity

to such an everything
a sea might represent

burning
with hunger

anger
to speak

the lines of a petal
unmake history

unmake this furniture of words
lying together

in the uninvented dark
by the true fire

the terrible weapon
of the flower

defeated
madness of the flower

raging in the mind
like earth before the seed dreams into root

its empty tunnels like a thought
that carries no message

falling through the mind in flames
the city becomes itself

hands become words become laws
for hands to use

against the fire
alight in the forest

time cuts down like an army
like a captured weapon

any man can fire
time the occupied city

besieged by memory
where will we go?

where this fire flutters
into mouths

to name the smallest things
discarded by the city of words

grassblades spring back like a crowd
waking one by one where we move on

single pieces in the constant motion
of this piercing forest

memory
that we would make live again

to renew our fear
by entering

the heart's glass mouth
its repetitious failure

to bring an image into daylight
we return to death

our apologies and imperfect songs
where to be poor is torment

to be rich is torment
black galleries sealed behind us

where light weeps without body
and all our promises

sealed in a catacomb with their tongues cut out
our companions on the staircase

frozen in the throat of death
and we their future voice

silent
among videos

the mind of the line
leading us into its swarf

its ride on the infinite wall of death
passing leaves passing water

passing the song entombed in water
passing the volumes of this song

passing a single page from these
passing its song like a tree among others

where we lie
our faces on the song's fibre

dreaming at the edge
of an eye

alight in the forest
we peer down like children at a pool

at all our loves' slow dumbshow
promising equal worlds

neglecting the city for love
of waves

of wind in the high trees raging like fire
softly around us

nevertheless it waits
to be happening next

the city waits
with its bird's eyes

its forest of hands
what should we fear there?

the night shields us
like a black lake

from glass eyes
the screen that sucks its graphite laws

in rooms
between death and death

waiting
without folklore or family

to remember the reason for waiting
for what is to come

can only be endured
with the roughness of leaves

remembered
black cathedral

of cedars
holding their seance above us

and the fire
of all this fuel

of all this darkness
like a black wine

a black scent
of everywhere arriving

our future
fixed by flame

with the shapes of all things in it
abandoned

by the drag of clocks
by the slag of hours

we labour to climb
to find our pain

waiting like a circus
all this is only us

and changeable
as a dream

we wait to dream
our predictions

grounded in inaccurate predictions
no place or ground

without the facts of war
infecting each island

the city great as darkness
as water

in the leaf itself
two worlds

of loss and torment
only listening again

will join
only watching

again the naked earth's examples
carry time

from one world to another
like a tree of blood

inside us
will join

in time's supple passing
no enemy again

and in the long roots of ocean
beginning beside us

the friendship of time
its miles of light

and this fire
our only machine

fixed in time
what shall we build

when time moves in our senses?
we lose our shape there

dream of rhythm
held in the hand like a flower

or the pollen from a flower
our shape there

water
measured

by images
their separation

leading here
to a glass of water

left on the windowsill
so far from one-another

silver bubbles in the glass
the moorland's silver horizon

wherever you are
the fibres of light beginning then

by the fire
the darkness around it

beginning then
and before then

the place within this place
the meeting point

a black flower
time's gold hand reaching through its heart

part 9 *body lyrics*

the city exhales its silver mask

                                        velocity of porticoes crumbling
                                        velocity of cobblestones wearing down

heat shimmers off the black felt

                        I am opening the water
                        under more blue than an eye
                        can circle
                        there
                                high up
                        a dandelion seed
                        spies me

                        a dragonfly passes close
                        I cross
                        warm veins
                        in the water

the comforting sound of trains

a sprinkler chirps like a cicada
on a grid of new turf

and we above the birds
only the swifts go higher

old broken people
like people carefully baked in an oven
like people carefully shattered
and re-inserted into bags of skin

with long grey hair
straight-backed behind his paunch
a beggar with two hats
one on his head
the other empty

(in the market asparagus
like boxes of finger bones)

fruit protest!
insurgence of flowers!
green
      purple
clouds of broccoli
the colrabi have landed in herds
with green antlers

a gallery where we eat the sculptures

morning
church bells

here is the body without affection
has it legs?
has it grey
the body is rust-coloured
at its entrances
the body is cured
like tobacco
voices circle it
like blind birds

no one will buy the body
is it sleeping?
it behaves like cloth
fallen
no one folds the body
it is unwearable
who shrunk it?
who is its enemy?
nobody
less than a cloud
less than a rumour
terrifying
and out of tempo

the body has surrendered
its enemy plays in it like fire

the body moves
infecting its enemy with amnesia

the body looks
it just looks
recording its empty census:
coin
bell
bread
bed
stone
the body consumes its own forgetfulness
like a lake under rain

the body's hieroglyph is discovered
I am hungry and homeless
no one can read it
not even the body

which ceases to look
perfecting its emptiness like a statue

sleep body
the poem loves you

a dead cannibal face
the eyes like those in a dead fish
the face set in its fat and tanned
with deep folds under the eyes
waits to eat the shop assistant
while she serves us

dust of reconstruction
the builders shout and joke
in their street-theatre of work
in ugly old clothes
bad haircuts
and yellow boots
saddled with tools and the arrogance
of rodeo stars

what can the trees remember?
everything
       forgotten kindergarten
defunct bureaucrat
the quiet disappearance of people
the loud reappearance of change
the cracked plaster loses all its teeth
woken from decay

and what are the ants doing?
all their effort leaves the dry grass random
as it was
here's one like a man
dragging a flagpole on a ploughed field

a woodlouse wanders through
a cow without a field
a stupendous vehicle
a button

I draw a circle round a fly
it pauses

here is the body without exits
an exposition of tubing
a lecture
it has discovered a language nobody speaks
speaks it:
no birds in the forest
dead radios
pinned on a busy runway

the body is a field something is ploughing
the body is a field someone is burning
who is its enemy?
not time
and all its doorways

surrounded not by silence
but a disbelief in sound
flowers grow instantly by the body
roaring like the arse of a jet

the body echoes with proverbs
its trap fills with grieving bulldozers
with klaxons and carillons

the body shines its silence
like a night sky
like a bright tile
left high on a ruin

what word does it use
to weigh the universe?
the bells are thrown in a great storm
though the bell-tower cannot hear it

here is the body without language
weaker than a bird
colder than a bell

the body pretends to wait
somebody moves it
the body dances
shivering and waiting

dead names the size of buses
pass the body travelling
from continent to continent:
take a Tom Cruise
use a Madonna
smoke The Whales
Coke washes whiter

the body rolls in fire
execrating curtains
gates and climbing plants
telephones the talking clock
and curses it

the body savages cities
writhing like a fish in the dust
somebody locks it up
somebody finds its language
to sentence it

                              at last the body laughs:
                              it has recognised a flower
                              through the wire

an insole
like a smoked tongue
six pieces of jigsaw
the city groaning
and clicking its bones

two huge poplars whisper
over the playground
like the sky's egg timers

the roly-poly man rolls past again
in his red tie

and here
his white cap the same style
as all those Germans wore in Frank Sinatra movies
or chasing Steve McQueen to the wire
slim and upright smoking
and reading a notice about bells
his clean bike propped behind him
a survivor

a boy's football bounces up the steps
the wino traps it
and passes it back
pleased with his work

by the library the bronze nude
has turquoise spraypaint nipples
and a label on her head

a boy climbs up to read it
thumps her smooth hair once or twice

                    here is the body that outlived a nation
                    what secrets it carries
                    like a box of seed
                    or an old-fashioned hat
                    its face like a field
                    where many are buried
                    still no theory can out-smile it

                    the body is its own bomb
                    its own bomb disposal
                    a dancing bomb
                    a bomb buying avocados
                    careful and disobedient and invisible
                    to grieve in three languages
                    only for bodies it has learnt
                    on overcast mornings in the highrise
                    maybe

it can end the world
and won't
walking slowly past the yellow banks
sometimes mumbling
mostly upright and miraculous

it has fed the poem
played the poem its favourite music
given the poem its grandchildren
their wide wise eyes

if the poem lived for a thousand years
they could never be enemies

        here's the censor
        adjusting his glasses
        dismantling his two pipes
        he wants our compassion
        for his use of reason
        the crowd of words he keeps alive
        restricted reasonably
        to certain uses
        in his glass case
        his armistice jacket

        outside the stones
        soaked with what he cannot use
        shine in a light rain

        it's early morning
        the words are hidden
        like thieves in the blossom

        they've consulted nobody
        and leap like butterflies onto the buildings

skateboarders enter the square
like swimmers at a pool
they arrive and dive in sweeping noisy arcs
across the pavings
and roll back to the steps
to step from their boards
easily and at walking pace

in one motion
like experienced fishermen
stepping from a boat

in her cool shop
the florist weaves a bunch of flowers
like someone beginning a coracle
like someone who can write
with twenty pens

the windows look at railway lines
and a dusty yard stacked with lumber

two old brown stoves intact
but the ceiling fallen in the kitchen

people grew old here
neither content nor defeated

a tall birch fills the back windows
empty shingle on the railway

the squatters won't move in
they want better
they couldn't care less
for the habits of the dead
clear in every colour and bad repair
an entire country
reduced to four rooms

down a path the garden
flanked by parked trucks
has crimson roses among bindweed
and a black cat

sharp breath of cars on the flyover

we have interrupted the caretaker
in his porkpie hat
levering old crates apart
to stack for winter

here is the walking body
what is it like?

two kids spit at the corner
comparing their gobs
it sees them
an Alsatian with a chewed stick
keeps pace with it a few paces
the body enjoys itself a little
alone and able
to move
lost in its mysterious torment
what is it like?

the body is like other bodies
leaving one-another
throughout the universe
heads down in doorways
made of undiscovered metal
that sounds when struck
it passes softly in its dead mine
it passes clanging in its cold furnace
it runs its eyes across builder's sand
what is it like?

no one can gentrify the body
whatever it learns
it is made for passage
mysterious torment
of shoes and fantasy

begins with rain
and swifts scything grey-paper sky

point by point the roofs darken
in the distance a tired siren

flowers punched by drops from the gutters
stormfall
the sealed cars pass
our coats go skewbald

(you're there
in her face for a moment
before I realise

then I try to find your face
what is there to say?
you can't answer
only I must imagine your answers
so you live
in my effort
the task you left me)

on its languid trampoline of water
the bike becomes beautiful
its mudguard a green bow
one pedal a green harmonica

caught in its collision with the river-bed
turning left
its metal turning into skin

new lilies ride the water
white yachts at anchor

a thin
    small
slow old lady in a blue headscarf
a grey coat
like a sleepy fly walking on the empty window
of asphalt

at the edge of the window
a torrent of cars

she comes to the edge of her world
it shrinks around her to an island

now she is a folded statue
staring past the edge of the world
the world ending behind her

                                  here is the body dreaming

                                  it is writing a story
                                  but each full-stop is the size of a lake
                                  the body reverses a moon's distance
                                  now it can read the earth
                                  who wrote it?

                                  the body writes the world
                                  like a child
                                  the world resembles the world
                                  but is also the body:

nine windows
eyes that must be fed
spacious and hairy

the body dreams backwards
it is a swan
pondering the swan beneath it
how can it return to itself?
long streets long trees
and flowers on the balconies
the body suffers the sickening parallax
of slow-moving trams
it concentrates on waltzing:
no luck

but the body has plans
no matter ants have covered them
the body reverses a moon's distance
now it can read the city

the body draws the city like a child
it always draws the city like a child

someone decided on a circus tent
so the musicians play there
it's their job
but they don't like it

the audience love it
they've made their choices:
comfortable clothes
a meal maybe
nothing will deflect them

a young mother in bright clothes
dances with her baby
at the entrance to the tent
she can see the music there
in its aquarium
the tenor flailing on his horn
like a predator on a golden fish

prostitutes along the park
standing regularly spaced
between parked cars
the trees behind them dark
under mauve sky

in there bodies change
these women change them

here is the body of Orpheus
a field of high grass
a white butterfly on a poppy
silent and a long
way away

the wind unites them
parts them
re-unites them
like the thoughts of a lover
the body sounds and sings
ecstatic and unhappy

the Orpheus that speaks
the *poet* Orpheus
is buried here
falling into himself like a river
like a river into a bigger river
his eyes like seeds
like newborn animals
the world rains on

such a country beside him
the women
lovely women
he searched for his own wound
the cities he catalogued
the faces he raged for
as far from him
as his own hand in sleep

                              his body has been stolen by his dreams
                              and walks among ruins
                              searching for a way out of the earth

beyond the city another city
and beyond a bigger city

a duck eating scattered sweetcorn
on the grass the backbone
and hind-legs of a hare

cubicles of air passing
the rule of the right-angle
over that which imagined it

rain drops on the page
on my hands like quick little tongues
small percussion in the chestnut

the mauve convulvulus arriving
like flowers forced
from a pipe of ink

two men working on the old teahouse
push water from tarpaulins
and make the entrance a white curtain
the waitress offers them a beer
wonderful she says wonderful

a radio
occasional hammering
an old man shuffles his feet on the grit
feeling at home

a frond of convulvulus
leans the back of its hand
on his shoulder

a white birch high on the ruin
in an arch that catches the prevailing wind
talking

the use for this place is past
though its round walled pond has stayed
swaying black and gentle
to soothe the city in the mind
when was it made?
too long ago to part us
the birch says so
shaking its costume

gold light knifes the forest
it's still
a squirrel
        moves

soft paths
to soothe the city in the mind
distract it with statues
where two paths cross
four stone fools
wearing no clothes to hunt
wearing no clothes to plough
to soothe the city in the mind
an underfed warrior
holding a short sword
falls in the churchyard

a moorhen tuts obsessively on the water
dragging her rope of light

rain powders the lake
the fish respond
enter its fading chains

a swallow turns
at head height on the air
flexing her tail like a ballerina
turning on one foot

swifts gather high above the house
circling and calling
they can't fall or break
the endless spring that powers them

(they must sleep trembling
like small engines
ticking over all night)

they chase each other
just because they can

a single silver plane
rules a white line high above them

                                            here is the body without destination
                                            watching the long barges pass
                                            where are they going?
                                            secure in their unfavourable element
                                            slowly
                                                    anywhere
                                            always

                                            the body is an empty barge
                                            a ruined cargo
                                            nothing fills it
                                            nothing steers it
                                            not even longing

on the far side of the water
one white eye of the city
watches over distant trees
where is the city's secret hidden?

how slowly time passes by the water
the body is far from everywhere
but the city will reclaim it
lead it back to the chain
or rain will drive it under cover

the body has forgotten everything
and remembered it again
and again:
too much science
better to watch the barges out of sight
wait for their wake
to knock on the jetty

the body will steal what it needs
the body will eat when it is hungry

soft dusk again
the houses forgiven by light
rain scatters accents in the sycamores

                        here is the body
                        possessed of infinity
                        its own blood passing under its face
                        like shadow over sand dunes

                        the body burns calmly
                        it can even walk
                        in the fat rain
                        in the green light of the archway
                        where can it go?
                        nowhere is everywhere
                        without some kind of love:
                        the eyes of stone that rain uncovers
                         the birch nervously holding out its hearts

                        the body sits in the light
                        like a broken palace
                        the body sits in the light
                        like a harp of gold

clear sky above the city
for the different journeys of birds
the talking crows
impatient swifts
and pigeons flying together
in one direction

shadows
and flat gold planes
of apartment blocks
above the roofs
a woman and a scottie dog
stand apart waiting
in an avenue of low trees

the body is a web of savours
an unbreakable weaving
frayed into the world
at its surface infinite journeys start
infinite messages arrive
and pass:
the body is architecture houses worship
how were they taken hostage?

the body
that narrator
knows more than we think
knows the strangeness
of others we long for and detest
knows all worthlessness
and wants to live

the body and the sky
created cities
dreaming each other
surface to surface
from this smoke
from this steam
invention of music
and freedom

I was a giant and slept in the rain
I was rain
and could not fathom my absorption
I was a giant breathing in the tree tops
I was a tree
attempting hand after hand
I was a hand
searching for the glove of freedom
I was freedom and motherless
I was a giant standing in the ocean
I was an ocean with imperfect thorns
I was a giant weeping over catkins
I was a giant calling out
I was a forest stronger than a giant
my intimate listening stronger than a giant
I was a river who could not stop

I was a giant lost in the rush-hour
I was a city falling to its death
armies fighting over all my gardens
armies fighting for my every window
I was a giant caged by a window
I was a window dreaming of stars

a feeling of somewhere familiar
never found
whose are the statues and the trees?

curves of light on the tunnel floor
creeping forward in a fuss of air
bewilderment hidden behind Raybans

sun paints the plane trees
generous fractures on the avenues
hor d'oeuvres under flightpaths

beside this city
the city of those who love

white light folding
slowly on the river
angels pass with gold on their western faces
some embrace
some carry angel babies
murmuring tongues

the body walks and looks
reprieved for the length of a street
where leaves fall

if not for us
whose is the city?
if not for love
to keep the rain from lovers

trees reach for the house
and light slides from their leaves

like ghosts
they listen
rain arrives
the wood an open ear
its intricate snare
blazing softly

soft dusk again
zig-zag of voices
candles each on their hesitant disk
of shadow

                                        I was a giant who broke the sun

rain increases its applause
and fades

the river brings more waves
it is never tired of waves